Blue Yonder

by Kate Aspengren

SAMUEL FRENCH

FOUNDED 1830

NEW YORK HOLLYWOOD LONDON TORONTO

SAMUELFRENCH.COM

ISBN 978-0-573-69900-9   Printed in U.S.A.   #29717

MUSIC USE NOTE

Licensees are solely responsible for obtaining formal written permission from copyright owners to use copyrighted music in the performance of this play and are strongly cautioned to do so. If no such permission is obtained by the licensee, then the licensee must use only original music that the licensee owns and controls. Licensees are solely responsible and liable for all music clearances and shall indemnify the copyright owners of the play and their licensing agent, Samuel French, Inc., against any costs, expenses, losses and liabilities arising from the use of music by licensees.

IMPORTANT BILLING AND CREDIT
REQUIREMENTS

All producers of *BLUE YONDER* *must* give credit to the Author of the Play in all programs distributed in connection with performances of the Play, and in all instances in which the title of the Play appears for the purposes of advertising, publicizing or otherwise exploiting the Play and/or a production. The name of the Author *must* appear on a separate line on which no other name appears, immediately following the title and *must* appear in size of type not less than fifty percent of the size of the title type.

BLUE YONDER was first produced at the Illinois Shakespeare Festival on August 3, 1998. The performance was directed by Bill Jenkins, with sound by Colleen Kenny and lighting by Patrick M. Leahy. The production stage manager was Daren A. C. Carollo. The cast was as follows:

PEOPLE PERSON	Carrie Lee Patterson
DYNAMITE	Tandy Cronyn
INNOCENTS	Kate Jordan
EVERYTHING YOU NEED	Annmarie Benedict
SPARE PARTS	Erin Schneider
BLUE YONDER	Deb Heinig
FOLLOWER	Tandy Cronyn
PLAYING THE GAME	Ali Balong
MAMA'S HERE	Lori Adams
TOUCHSTONE	Tandy Cronyn

BLUE YONDER was subsequently produced by The University of Iowa, September 3-6, 1998. The director was Kate Aspengren. Lighting and scenic design was by Pip Gordon. The costume designer was Joyce McKinley, and Gwen Komala was the sound designer. The stage manager was Tina Shackleford. The cast was as follows:

PEOPLE PERSON	Katharine Guthrie
DYNAMITE	Tandy Cronyn
EVERYTHING YOU NEED	Rachael Lindhart
SPARE PARTS	Mary Fons
TAURUS THE BULL	Rachael Lindhart
BLUE YONDER	Tandy Cronyn
FOLLOWER	Tandy Cronyn
INNOCENTS	Katharine Guthrie
PLAYING THE GAME	Mary Fons
MAMA'S HERE	Rachael Lindhart
TOUCHSTONE	Tandy Cronyn

The monologue "Heat" was added later and was not a part of these original productions.

CONTENTS

PRODUCTION NOTE

The monologues in *Blue Yonder* may be performed in any order and with
any number of actors.

ACKNOWLEDGEMENTS

Thank you to Mary Lou Aspengren, Leanne Chandler, Tandy Cronyn,
Sarah Douglas, Joanne Grey, Kelli Grey, Susan Goodner, Bill Jenkins,
Bev Klug, Michelle Ladd, Tina Shackleford, Marcy Levy Shankman,
Jeffrey Sweet, Trina Tjersland, the Iowa Summer Writing Festival, and
the Illinois Shakespeare Festival.

And especially to Rachel Henderson Falls, whose work with the initial
development of this play was invaluable.

for Kelli

PEOPLE PERSON

(**DIANE** *wears a telephone headset. The phone rings.*)

Good morning. Employment. *(pause)* We have a website for our job listings. It's www...oh, I see. In that case, you can also access our list of available jobs through our recorded job announcement line. That number is 253...no, you have to call the recording. That number is 2...no, I cannot give you the information. That is why we have the recording. That number is...*(She winces. The caller has apparently slammed the phone down.)* You're welcome.

(The phone rings.)

Good morning, employment. Yes. We have a recording that lists our job openings. That number is 253...oh, a specific job. Yes, I can give you information on a specific job. Which job are you interested in? Um-hm. *My* job? How do you get this particular job? That's what you're asking? Um-hm. Oh, you're a people person? I see. Well...why not? Listen closely.

You start when you're nine or ten. You're in the fourth grade and Mrs. Mack says that everyone has to give a speech about what they want to be when they grow up. And it's the day of the speeches and you've worked so hard on yours, you've practiced in front of the full-length mirror in your parents' bedroom, you've even traced pictures out of the Encyclopedia Britannica to use as visual aids. You are ready and you know your speech will be the best one in the room and – I *am* telling you! Just listen! This is valuable information that I am sharing! So you sit through Michael Merrill's speech about being a veterinarian and Eddy Ackerman talks about being a race car driver and somehow manages to avoid using any words with more than a single syllable. You don't see how you can sit still for one more speech.

But it's Sally Cooper's turn next and she does this brown-nosing speech about how she wants to be a teacher just like Mrs. Mack and the other kids smirk and shake their heads, but you don't join in because you are next and you know you're going to blow Sally and Michael - and certainly the monosyllabic Eddy-right out of the water.

So it's your turn and you're in front of the class and you begin. "My plan is to be a traveler through time. I want to wake up with the Cro-Magnon children, have lunch with Benjamin Franklin, and eat supper with Marie Curie. And then I want to go to the future and fly to other planets and meet the creatures who live on Mars and Jupiter." (You'd planned to say Mars and Uranus until you realized the folly of saying "Uranus" to a room full of fourth-graders.) You take a long, meaningful pause and you look up because you know this is the best beginning to any speech, ever. But Mrs. Mack has this worried look and the kids...the kids are laughing at you like they did with Sally Cooper. You take a deep breath and go on. You show your drawings of the first Thanksgiving and of the men who dug the Suez Canal and of Amelia Earhart. By the end of the speech the other kids are laughing right out loud, and Mrs. Mack isn't even trying to stop them. And when you go back to your seat, Bradford Martin sticks his foot out in the aisle and when you stumble over it he says, "Look. She took her first trip!" And everybody laughs really loud.

Mrs. Mack gives you a 'D' on the assignment because she feels you didn't take it seriously. She would have given you an 'F' except that she was impressed with those tracings from the Encyclopedia Britannica.

Then...Hey! Do you want to know how to get this job or not? Then let me finish.

You go off to college. By now you've abandoned the time traveler idea. You end up as a social work major. It wasn't exactly your first choice but it makes sense. After all, you are a people person.

You finish up your degree. Your Bachelor of Arts degree in social work. You are now a certified people person. You start working as a social worker. And it turns out you're pretty good at it. But it's only your clients who think so. Your supervisor thinks you have a lot to learn. You stay up until midnight holding the hand of a pregnant fourteen year-old and later you get in trouble because now other clients – other *people* – might expect that you are available to them after normal office hours. It's a dangerous precedent and one that cannot be condoned. Your supervisor is also dubious about your future because you've been known to wear jeans while practicing social work. Apparently denim and compassion cannot co-exist.

You work there for couple of years and then you move on. Because you know if you don't move on soon, you're going to be asked to go because of your wardrobe and the annoying way in which your clients seem to like and trust you. You know that you'll miss the clients very much, and you are grateful to them for all they've taught you, but you also know that you are on thin ice with the administration. So you go on to another job. A social worker again because, after all, you are still a people person.

And this one works out rather well, and you even get along with this supervisor who actually wears jeans herself. And you and the supervisor start to become friends and you get closer and closer, and she likes your work and you start to feel good about life and about yourself. Hey! I can hear you turning pages! Put that magazine down and pay attention! One night your supervisor, who is by now also your friend, says, "If I wasn't married, I think we would have become lovers a long time ago." And you don't know what to say to that. Because, sure, you find her attractive and there were times when you thought she was flirting with you but she's married so you've always assumed that what you thought was flirting was simply collegiality. And a couple of days later, in the ladies' room, she gives you the tiniest of kisses. You enjoy it but you mention the fact that she's married and that you're seeing someone new and that all of this is making you very uncomfortable. She tries to persuade you, but you stand your ground. A week later she calls you into her office and she says that they're not very happy with your work and that they'll give you the option of resigning or being fired. But, by the way, she'd still like to be friends. And you don't know what to say. You panic. You think resigning is better than being fired so you quit. And you feel like you've been hit by a rather large and fast-moving truck. You hurt all over and you know that something isn't right here. But you're young and in pain and you simply don't know what to do. So you don't do anything.

You look around for other jobs. Jobs where you don't have to put your heart right there on the desk every day next to your stapler and your date stamp. That's how you find this one. And you spend your day listening to other people tell how they need to find themselves, how they are sure the right job will make them the person they dream of being. And you know that a different job won't help at all. But you smile and take their application and record the score of their typing test. Even though you're smiling, you don't let yourself care about them. They'll get a job or they won't. It's none of your business, none of your concern. You decide to be a people person after five o'clock. You have friends and you laugh and smile and talk – but not during working hours. You think that this isn't so bad, you can do this for twenty, thirty years, the rest of your life. So you aren't looking around, you are not actively seeking employment. Although when the job listings come out sometimes you take a little peek just to see if there might be something listed under the heading of "Time Traveler."

But there never is.

And that's how you get a job like mine. Now is there anything else I can help you with?

DYNAMITE

*(**DANIELLE** is in her mid-thirties. She wears a red satin shirt tied at the waist and shorts.)*

It's not so hard as it looks – gettin' blown up by the dynamite.

It's not so bad.

The way I first got the idea was that I saw this guy do it one time. At a stock car race over in Oskaloosa? He got in this box and BAM! The dynamite went off and people cheered and clapped and he took a real big bow like some kinda opera singer. He even dressed like one. In a tux and bow tie and all.

Now, the box he used was made outa cardboard. Cardboard painted to look like wood. My boxes – they're Styrofoam. White Styrofoam sheets held together with that silver duck tape.

What I do is this.

First I go out and look around the field, make sure that everything is okay. But usually it is because they try to keep all the glass and the stuff that could cut you away, on account of how it could hurt the ball players and all.

I like to get blown up right on home plate.

A couple of places they won't let me do that. Say it's too close to the spectators. But, hell, I'm right there in the box and the spectators got about a twenty foot wall of diamond chain link fence in front of 'em. If somebody gets hurt it ain't gonna be some guy in the stands.

But a couple of ball teams, they make me do it in the outfield. It's just not the same. It's quieter and not so dramatical. But I gotta do what they say if I wanna work there.

So anyways I check out the field. I don't wear my costume then. I wear red coveralls that got these crossed sticks of dynamite embroidered on the back. My mom did the embroidery. She is very talented at arts and crafts.

If everything checks out, I give the high sign to the guys in back. They carry my box out. They carry it on a big rectangle of two sheets of one inch CX plywood nailed together at the corners. I use two sheets because at first I only used one and I accidentally took a piece out of home plate over in Springfield. They nearly had a fit and said they had to replace the whole thing before they could even play. Practically caused a riot 'cause folks were pissed that the game hadn't started. So now I use two sheets of wood. The guys carryin' the box set it down and I make sure that it's all level. Then I put the charge inside and I check that everything is just so. I step back for one last look and I go off to my trailer to put on my costume. It's neon pink and green with a green cape. My mom made it too, but I chose the colors.

Before they announce me they play that song from *2001, A Space Odyssey. (She hums the first part of it.)* Then the guy on the PA, he says, "Ladies and Gentlemen, it's the Dynamite Woman! Miss Danielle Wise!" And I walk out onto that ball field. I walk out in time to the music. And I walk up the first base line and back. Then I walk up the third base line and back. Then, just as the music is finishing, I stand right there at home plate and I lift my arms up – real slow – so that at the end I am there with my arms up high and my cape flying in the wind.

While I take off my cape, the PA guy is talking about how the charge is big enough to blow up a safe. Then I put on my helmet. It's red with a sparkle finish and it has my initials – D.W. – right in the front in gold letters. I crawl into the box and the PA guy is saying how dangerous it is and how people with small children and heart conditions should probably leave. Actually I don't think it would hurt them. But it makes it all more scary-like.

When I'm in the box, I give the thumbs-up and they put the lid on.

Then the PA guy starts the countdown.

THREE – I'm layin' real still, not movin', so I don't accidentally kick out the side of the box. I did that one time. The box fell apart and just ruined the whole effect.

TWO – My hand is on the button. I'm ready. I'm ready. ONE – My finger pushes down.

Afterward I hear the applause. The cheerin'. Sometimes the concussion makes me black out for just a second. But then I get up. They're whistlin' and cheerin' and there's still little bits of Styrofoam floatin' around in the air like confetti.

I pull off my helmet. I raise my hand up in the V for victory. And I wave to them all. All of them, standin' up for me.

The Dynamite Woman.

It's a real good feelin'.

TAURUS THE BULL

(**SADIE** *is in her 70s. She wears a long blue coat with many gold buttons and much braid. She wears black leather gloves and black snow boots.*)

Good morning, Mr. Hanes. You're up and at 'em early this morning. *(She waves after him.)* You have a nice day now, you hear.

Thirty-two years. Right here. Same doorway. Different door. Been through five or six of 'em in thirty-two years. Replaced the tile two different times. Repainted the foyer – oh, geez – repainted the foyer probably a dozen times. Mostly been this off-white color like now. Snow white once. Didn't last long, you know – fingerprints and scuff marks all over. You can imagine. Painted it mint green twice. Glad to see that go – both times.

Good morning, folks. Button up now – wind's getting fierce.

Seventy. *(pause)* Oh, I know you're wondering. Everybody does. I'm obviously not some college girl. Seventy in April. The 27th. Taurus the Bull. *(She holds up both fists, suddenly fierce.)* Don't mess with me! *(She drops her fists and laughs.)* Oh, I'm just kidding you. Don't wet yourself.

I'm here every – excuse me. Mrs. Young! Welcome home! How was Spain? My goodness, you look so rested. Nice to have you back. I'll send your bags right up.

Mrs. Young sent me postcards from her trip. Oh, I get 'em from everyplace you can think of – Portugal, Japan, London. Phoenix. They all seem to think that I need to know what's going on every minute of their lives. They bring me gifts, too. It's generous of them, sure, but how many of those straw baskets from the Bahamas does one woman need?

Mrs. Berkowitz! We haven't seen you out and about for a long time. You have a nice day.

Funny part of it is they've got no notion of the places I've seen. Belgian Congo. Thailand-only it was called Siam in those days. Sailed around Cape Horn and rode on a train through Russia. Even took a walk along the Great Wall of China once. Oh, I've been all over. One good thing about having parents who were missionaries. Join the church and see the world! *(She laughs.)* So I don't tell 'em where I've been. I just thank them for their refrigerator magnet that's cut in the shape of Italy or the seashell nightlight they brought me from Maui. But I don't tell 'em where I've been. I don't think they want to know.

Now, before you even ask this, it doesn't make any difference that I'm a woman. Not to me, at least. Doesn't take a man to open a door, does it? If it did, women wouldn't get anywhere. Just sit inside all the time waiting for some man to open the door.

So I'm a doorman. Big deal. Big whoopie as my granddaughter says. Big old whoopie.

Every now and then a tourist will spot me. Take a picture. Ask me to pose with their Aunt Fanny or something. I do it. Even though it kinda irks me. Makes me feel like Minnie-the-Mouse at Disneyland. Like the bearded lady at the circus. Some people get all gushy like they think it's cute to see an old lady done up in a doorman's uniform. Tell you one thing: old isn't cute. It's just old.

One woman called me spunky. I hated hearing that. Sounds like something you'd call a pug dog. I said to her, "Hey you – I might be small but so is a firecracker!" It sounded good at the time but I guess all it did was help to prove her point.

Didn't take the job to be on display. Took the job to have a job. My husband worked. I worked. Difference is, I still do. He retired, but I'm not quite ready.

A job is a job is a job. Some of them you stand up, some of them you sit down. A job is a job is a job. And this woman thing. Women are in the police. Women drive buses. Who says they can't open doors? Sure it gets hard sometimes. When you've got some drunk sleeping in the entry and you have to boot him out. Hell, I had a guy die right out here once. Took the city three hours to haul him away. You think that wasn't a problem? Think that didn't make the people in my building a little edgy? Every job's got its difficulty. I just take it as it comes.

Morning, Dr. Edwards! Looks like it's gonna be another cold one. Say, thank you for that wooden tray from the Philippines. Yes, real monkey pod. It certainly is special. You have a good day. I'll see you when you get home.

Yes, sir. I'll be standing right here when you get home.

SPARE PARTS

(**CHRISTINE** *is dressed in a gray sweatshirt and jeans.*
She is barefoot. She looks very tired.)

When I was born, my family called me the miracle baby and
my picture was in *The New York Times*. I guess you could say
that I was famous. See, my big sister, Lisa, was sick. Dying.
With leukemia. The only thing that would save her was a
bone marrow transplant but they needed an exact donor.
The closest donors are brothers and sisters. Did you know
that? Lots of people don't know that. So when I was about
a year old they took my bone marrow from *(points)* right
here, in my hip – you can still see the little mark and gave it
to Lisa and she got well. Now she's married and has a little
baby and a real nice house. I was even her maid of honor.

A lot of people got mad at my parents. They wrote nasty letters to the newspapers and called up the TV stations. Said
my mom and dad only had me to save Lisa's life. That it
wasn't fair because I couldn't give my approval for them to
take out my bone marrow. But she's my sister, you know? Of
course I'd want her to live. Besides, I don't even remember
it so it couldn't have hurt that much, could it? I mean, if
something hurts you that bad, wouldn't you remember it?

When I was about fifteen, my grandpa needed a new
kidney. His just weren't working right and they said he was
poisoning himself from the inside. So I gave him one of
mine. You only need one kidney anyway. Did you know
that? You only need one kidney but you can't spare any
grandparents. That's what my family said.

Then last year my dad got sick. He had something wrong
with his lungs. I forget what it's called exactly but it was
pretty bad. So they asked me would I mind, you know,
giving up part of my lung for my Dad, and I said no, I

wouldn't mind. Not for my Dad. Of course, I wouldn't mind. Got a big scar from that one goes from here clear over to here *(runs finger from middle of chest to middle of back)* and sometimes I still can't sleep very well from the nerve spasms I get. He ended up dying anyway.

There was some other stuff too. Skin graft for my cousin, a teeny slice off the top of my liver for my sister's little baby. Couple of inches of vein from my leg for my grandma.

People don't understand why I do it. But it's my family, you know. If they need a little piece of me to keep them going, I'll give it to them. I can't tell them no if they're counting on me. Can I?

Sometimes in my room at night I take off my clothes and look at myself in the mirror on the back of the door. I touch all the scars. Take an inventory of my parts. I don't know what will be next; it's hard to say.

I think maybe this is my calling, you know. We're taught that everyone is here for a purpose and I think this must be mine. I mean, it has to be.

Because when I was born, my family called me the miracle baby and my picture was in *The New York Times*.

EVERYTHING YOU NEED

*(**COOKIE** wears a royal blue smock with "Woolworth"
embroidered on it. She also wears a big pin that says,
"MAY I HELP YOU?")*

There's an awful lot to be said for finding everything you
need in one place. That's the way Woolworth's is. Get all
your heart's desires met in one shopping trip.

I'd see folks come in on their lunch hour. Grab themselves
the turkey and dressing hot plate at the counter, pick up
some arthritis medicine for their mother-in-law, some toy
or other for their kid, and a couple of spools of thread. All
in the same hour. Not many places you can do that.

I always liked looking in people's shopping carts. Seeing
what they wanted. *(She looks over an imaginary cart and takes
an inventory of its contents.)* Dental floss, Phillips head screwdriver, Cadbury milk chocolate bar, birthday card, framed
picture of some football player. Then I'd try to make up a
little story about what they were fixing to do with all those
things. Maybe this person is having someone special over
for dinner and it's this special person's birthday – that
explains the card and maybe even the framed picture if the
person is a man. It's not the kind of picture a woman would
enjoy as a gift. Or they might have themselves a water mark
on the wallpaper or a place where somebody hauled off
and stuck a fist through the wall. They could be planning
to cover up that bad spot with this picture. The screwdriver
is to tighten up a wobbly leg on the table, the chocolate
bar is what they're planning to serve for dessert-probably
cut up in little slices. And the dental floss...the dental floss
is because if you're having dinner with somebody special
you do not want to have tuna casserole caught between
your teeth.

I play that same game when I'm at the grocery, but it's harder. Not as much variety. Yesterday, over to the Food City, I was behind some lady with nothing in her cart but eight gallons of milk and a watermelon. Not much to make out of that. Except they sure do like their milk.

Been here for thirty-three years now. Sounds like a long time. It all goes so fast though. Spent the first seven years at the candy counter. Serving up caramel turtles and chocolate-covered peanuts. That was my first job. My dad was so proud of me. He used to say that Woolworth's was a good, solid company and if I just put in an honest day's work then the store would treat me right. Sometimes those first couple of years I would look up from the candy counter and see my dad. Standing outside on the sidewalk and holding that flat straw hat of his in one hand. Just watching me work. And smiling.

I got promoted to notions. Didn't miss the candy counter. That sweet, chocolately smell can get right up in your nose and stay there. Makes you feel a little sick. I didn't mind moving to notions. I don't think many places have themselves a notions department anymore. Probably ninety percent of your people couldn't even tell you what notions means. It was thread, pins, zippers, buttons, that kind of thing. Also padded hangers for ladies clothes. Shoe trees. Little sachet packets for your dresser drawer. Working notions wasn't bad. Just not all that interesting. Hard to get worked up over a bobbin or a dress shield. So I was glad to move on.

Next I was assistant manager of the stationery department. I thought it would be easy just dealing with cards and pens and the like. Turned out to be a nightmare. People dig through those birthday cards, looking for just the right one, but they never put them back in the same place. Worse, they try to read the card without pulling it out of the little slot. Bend the corners down, then nobody will buy them. I'll tell you, I like people, I really do, but sometimes you have to wonder what in the world they are thinking about.

And the fall? I don't even like to think about the fall.
School supplies. Just hearing those two words makes me
want to break out in hives. You got two mothers fighting
over the same knapsack and some kid is crying because
he wants a pen that writes in green ink or all the lunch
buckets left have Superman on them and he wants a lunch
bucket with anybody on it except Superman.

Even when I was working in stationery, even then, I loved
coming to work. First thing in the morning is so nice,
everything lined up all neat and orderly. Things would get
pretty picked over by the end of the day but the evening
shift folks always stayed around after closing to get things
ship-shape again. I used to walk up and down the aisles,
just marveling at all we had here, at how nice it looked
before we unlocked the doors. Nail polish sorted out by
color: Peach Ice, Flamingo Pink, Big Apple Red. Candy
bars: Baby Ruths and Butterfingers and Cherry Mash –
each kind in its own little wire bin. Head scarfs all folded
up nice and neat, aspirin bottles turned around so the
labels faced front, fishfood shelf restocked. Can open-
ers, underpants, artificial flowers, squirt guns. Paperback
books, vacuum cleaner bags, mouthwash, key chains, spice
racks, hair curlers. Everything in its place.

People ask did I shop here myself. Well, of course. No
better shopping if you ask me, and I have been to plenty
of those malls so I do know what I'm talking about. Those
places are just like a big circus. Some of them even got car-
nival rides right inside. Exactly like a circus.

Woolworth always offered you just what you needed. Never
more. Those big places tease you with stuff you don't need,
don't even want.

Guess I must have spent a fair amount of my paycheck
right here in the store. They have these cookies – they're
imported from Denmark – and I've had my share of those
over the years. They're real buttery tasting and not too
hard. Come in big tins that have the flags of the world on
them. I suppose I had one of those cookies on every break
I took for the past thirty-some years. Always kept a tin in

my locker. Never got tired of them. That's how I got my nickname. It's due to all those cookies.

Besides the cookies, I always liked the foot powder we sell. It's a special Woolworth's brand and you find it right over by the Dr. Scholl's products. As many hours as I spend on my feet, I have to take care of them. I heard them interview one of those gals who runs in marathons. Talking about how she has to take good care of her feet because without them she's nothing. Same thing here. I spend the better part of eight hours standing up. And that's six days a week, sometimes all seven if somebody calls in sick. So I take mighty good care of my feet. Every morning I sprinkle some of that foot powder into my shoe. Then I pour some in my hand and rub it all over, rub it in good. It's medicated so it helps keep my feet from hurting. Sometimes they still get sore but not as much as without this powder. It's the medication in it that makes all the difference.

(She removes the button from her smock.)

Some things you just expect will always be there. You turn on the faucet, you expect water to come out. You visit the Grand Canyon, you assume nobody's filled it in with dirt since your last trip. It's always going to be there. That's what I figured about the Woolworth's. Been there since I was a little girl. Be there forever. But every now and then you get a surprise.

I don't know. Maybe somebody better check on the Grand Canyon. Make sure it's still there.

When the sale started, I bought myself a dozen tins of those buttery cookies and seven of those plastic shaker-things with the foot powder in them. I would have bought more but that was all we had left. (*She starts to remove her smock.*)

I've looked around, filled out some applications. It's funny, when they call me up or when it's my turn to go into the office for an interview, they always call me Evelyn because that's what I write on the form. Since it's my real name and all. Sometimes it takes me a minute. I don't know who they're talking to. On account of how I got called Cookie for so many years. Then I remember. And I think to myself, oh yeah. That's me. I'm Evelyn.

(She neatly folds the smock.)

I've been trying for jobs at other stores. Those placement people see thirty-odd years of retail on your application, and you can bet your booties you'll be going to lots of stores for interviews. Sent me to one at The Gap. I don't know what got in to them to send me there; everybody who works there is my niece's age. I just looked at them, handed back my application, and turned around and walked out of the store. Little girl who was the manager seemed real relieved.

Then they sent me to that WalMart. Man asked me what did I think of his store. I said, "I can tell you're trying, but you're no Woolworth." And that was the end of that interview.

The thing is you could find your heart's desire at a place like Woolworth. But finding something doesn't mean it's yours forever. Still, it's real good while it lasts.

BLUE YONDER

(**LU** *wears a battered leather aviator's jacket.*)

Here's what's going to happen. We start with the four basics. And if you don't know them now you damn well sure will when we get finished. Climbs, descents, turns, straight and level flying. Got it? From there we'll go on to slow flight and stalls. Listen up now – a stall doesn't mean your engine died. A stall in an airplane is not the same thing as stalling your car. We'll come back to that.

I'll be your flight instructor. I've been at this for fifteen years now, so you're in good hands. I've flown every kind of aircraft there is. Copters, gliders, military planes. Flown 'em all. Never met an aircraft I didn't like. And that didn't like me. Still got a few more I'd like to fly someday.

Now let's get one thing straight. Because I know you're going to ask. Happens every time. But if one more person asks me about Amelia Freakin' Earhart, I am going to puke. She married rich, had good P.R., and got herself lost. End of story. Of course, having a drunk for a navigator probably didn't help matters much either. There were lots of women who flew before Amelia Earhart and a whole bundle of them who flew after her. You just keep that in mind.

I always wanted to fly and Amelia Earhart didn't have anything to do with it. It's all I wanted when I was a kid. Probably the same thing for you, huh? One time I dreamed that I won a big contest and the prize was a trip to Florida. They came right to the school to pick me up, parked their plane - it was a Lockheed Constellation - parked their plane right there in the school parking lot! I got to climb into that big old Connie and sit up on the deck with the pilot. The other kids were waving and yelling. I was surprised how clear I could see from up there. Funny thing is, when I got up in the airplane to solo for the first time - and this was years later - when I got up there, the world looked exactly like it had in my dream.

So what we'll do is this: I'll talk you through our preflight. Make sure everything is ready to roll. We'll check the fuel, the oil. Run a finger along the edge of the prop to make sure there aren't any nicks. You can't take too much time doing this. Bolts, cotter pins, fasteners, moveable surfaces. The whole nine yards. It takes some time but it's absolutely necessary. Miss one little thing and you end up buying the farm. That means dying, if you don't already know it. Flying is like anything else. We've got our own language. Hell, there's a whole bunch of ways just to say somebody croaked. Fly west. Auger in. Punch a hole. Doesn't matter how you say it though. Dead is dead.

(An airplane flies over. She drifts away for a moment, thinking of something else. She snaps out of it abruptly.)

Anyhoo, if you've done your homework, you know all about lift and thrust and drag. You'd *better* know about them anyway. You know that lift is what keeps an airplane up. It's all about the air pressure flowing over and under the wing. You create that upward force and there you go. You're up in the air. You're flying. *(sings)* "Climbing high into the sun." When we were kids we used to try to get my Uncle Bill to sing the Air Force song. He was a radioman in a Flying Fortress in World War Two. He'd throw his head back, and shut his eyes, and belt out that song for all he was worth. I used to love to watch him sing it. Gave me goose bumps. Every time.

But you're not here to listen to stories about my relatives, are you? You're here to learn how to fly.

About the lessons…what I like to do is see people two or three days a week. Then we can work your ground school in on the days when it's not fit to fly. To be honest with you, we're going to have to play that by ear. I'm supposed to start some treatments. Medical procedures. Not sure how they'll affect me. But I'm planning to be here every day that I can. Lost the left one two years ago and I was back flying in no time at all. Flying's the only thing that got me through. Knowing that when it was all over I could get off the ground again. Now they say it's shown up again. Doesn't look so good. But I'll do what needs to be done so that I can be back here. I'm not the type to sit around in my nightgown feeling sorry for myself. I'd rather be flyin' than dyin'. That's my motto.

Jesus, Mary, and Joseph. I got myself right off the track. What the hell were we talking about before…? *(Thinks for a moment.)* Ah! Lift! So suppose you're climbing and the angle of your wing is increasing, you know. Like this *(She demonstrates with her hand.)* Pretty soon air can't flow over the wing and your lift is just shot to hell. You've got to make some corrections – add power, lower the nose – or you'll be in some deep, deep doo. First time you experience a stall, I guarantee you'll rate a full ten points on the pucker factor scale. Just you wait and see.

Like I said before, a stall doesn't have anything to do with engine failure. You can stall when you're at full power. Important thing is not to panic, to do what's necessary to get the air flowing over your wing again, and to keep on flying. That's all that counts.

You've just got to keep on flying.

FOLLOWER

*(**LILLA** is nicely attired in a very professional-looking navy blue power suit. She also wears expensive, but well-worn, running shoes.)*

I follow people. It's what I do.

I don't mean like I follow them for a block or two down the sidewalk until they go into Walgreens to buy shampoo or spearmint gum. Not like a little lost puppy or something pathetic like that.

I mean I really follow them. For days. Sometimes for whole weeks at a time.

I'm serious about this. Sometimes I call in to the bank and say I can't come to work that day because I have the stomach flu. Or an allergic reaction. But it's really so that I can follow one of my people. You can't quit following them just because you have to go to work. Because really this following thing is my work. It's my career, I guess you could say. My vocation. And I'm good at it, too.

Like this guy I've been following lately. C. Walters. I don't know his whole first name. I only read his mailbox and that's what it said. C. Walters. Could be Charles, I guess. He might be a Charles. Not a Chuck, though. No way is this guy a Chuck. But it might be Charles. Doesn't really matter though. So I just call him Clifton. It could be Clifton. I had an uncle named Clifton once.

So I started in following Clifton one day last week. Tuesday, I guess it must have been. No, wait, it was Wednesday. Wednesday last.

I always liked talking like that. Wednesday last. Instead of saying last Wednesday. It sounds sort of sophisticated or something. Like something Katharine Hepburn would say in a movie. Wednesday last.

Anyway, I started following Clifton – Wednesday last – because I saw him coming out of McDonalds and he was drinking his coffee through a straw. Hot coffee through a straw. I mean, the coffee could melt that straw. Then you have melted plastic swimming around in your blood system. Through your vital organs. Your liver and everything. Kill you sure as hell.

So I knew that I had to follow him.

You can't just follow anybody. Not if you're serious about it. Some of them just take off after the first person they see. That's just not the way it's done. You have to be real careful. Selective.

Like Rose Marie. Some other month ago I was waiting for a bus and two women got off. One of them was dressed real nice. Like for a birthday party or a funeral. She had on a sky blue dress with a white collar and a big white bow right in the front of it. I always liked that color - sky blue. It relaxes you, you know. Oh yeah, it's scientifically proven. You see a color like sky blue or dusty rose and you get all relaxed and comfy. But then you take a color like red or that bright orange color like the warning cones when they're fixing the street and everybody gets all agitated and angry. It's a fact.

Anyway, Rose Marie. In this particular instance I happened to know her name because when they got off the bus this other woman, who was wearing red by the way and making me very uncomfortable, this other woman said, "See you later, Rose Marie." I learned her name without even checking her mailbox. Sometimes it is that easy. So Rose Marie walks away from this woman in red who is by this time making me furious. Rose Marie walks off and I go off after her. Figuring she is going to a special event somewhere. She walks about a block and then sits down on one of the benches where you wait for the bus. It was yellow and had an advertisement for a mausoleum painted on it. Rose Marie sat down and reached into this straw bag she was carrying and took out a book. I couldn't tell what it was. Some big thick book. Not a paperback either. So I figured, okay.

She's waiting for a bus. But the thing is, I walked back and forth watching her and she never got up. For three hours she just sat there all dressed up and reading. Then she got back up, went down the street, met up with her friend, the red lady again, and got on the next bus. That's all she did. I watched her for three damn days and that's all she did. Came there all dressed up, sat on the mausoleum bench and read a book. Then she left. I quit watching her soon after that. What's the point?

I mean, you cannot follow someone unless they are going somewhere.

HEAT

*(**MICHELLE**, a firefighter, is dressed in turnout gear. The rest of her equipment lies at her feet. She is hot, dirty, and exhausted.)*

It's not the flame that burns you. It's the heat.

A simple party trick proves this. You light a candle and... *(passes hand through imaginary flame)* the flame can't hurt you. But hold your hand there longer and it'll begin to redden and sting. A while longer, the skin bubbles and blisters. The pain is intense. Beyond anything you've known. Beyond anything you thought possible.

If you could stand to keep your hand there long enough, the skin would char. The nerve endings would be destroyed and the pain would end. For good.

Stay in one place long enough and you'll burn. You can walk into the fire, but you need to learn to move through it. You find that's not as hard as it seems. You learn that you can take anything for a moment. You face the fire, you welcome it, you understand what it can do. And then you get out.

It's when you stay too long – when you linger – that you'll get hurt. The part of you that burns will never return and you'll be left with more scars and less feeling than you had before.

The only way to avoid this is to keep moving before the flames surround you and the fire walls you in. Before the heat cooks your flesh and makes your blood simmer. Before the fire takes away sensation and the smoke takes away your breath.

You must keep moving.

You must remember that it's not the flame that burns you. It's never just the blaze itself.

It's the heat.

(She wearily picks up her equipment and goes back to work.)

INNOCENTS

*(**GRACE** wears a cardigan sweater.)*

I am here by eight a.m. every morning. Monday through Saturday. Rain, shine, sleet, snow. I came here the morning after my oral surgery. I came here when my mother was dying of bone cancer and on the day of my sister's wedding. I came twice when there were tornado warnings and once I stood here during a blizzard that left us with eighteen inches of snow. I cannot imagine what it would take to keep me away.

I do this because I care about our young people, particularly our young ladies. I do this because I am a mother myself. But mostly I do this because it is God's will.

(shouts) "THE INNOCENT AND THE RIGHTEOUS SLAY THOU NOT – FOR I WILL NOT ACQUIT THE GUILTY!"

(She writes something in a small notebook.) J...A...H...one... four...six. Bree's husband works for motor vehicles. We give him these plate numbers and then he gives us a name and address. We write to the people who've been here, send along some literature and ask them to reconsider their decision. Or, if they've already been persuaded to have their child killed, we ask them to pray to the Lord for forgiveness and we offer them counseling. Of course, Dr. Meade is a gynecologist so sometimes women are just here for their yearly exams. And now and then it's someone who has miscarried. I understand that seeing the pictures might cause those women some pain and anguish. I am sorry for that, but we must continue to fight the good fight. Proverbs says there are seven things that are an abomination to God. One of these is hands that shed innocent blood. How could I not use any means possible to destroy something that is an abomination to God? Even it if does

cause the occasional bit of pain to someone else. All of us in our group are in agreement about that.

There are several of us who are regulars here. Bree, Mildred, Connie, Sister Bonaventure, Mrs. Moore. We've gotten to be just like a little family over the years. There is not much about one another that we don't know. Our bond grows deeper every time we persuade a young lady to turn away from the doors of this killing center. There is such a celebration whenever that happens. I do not know a feeling like the one I get when I keep another baby away from the executioners. I think of it as saving another little lamb for Jesus.

Sunday afternoons we get the whole group together and have a little prayer meeting right outside of Dr. Meade's house. He lives over in the Heights. Real nice area. First we go in and pass out leaflets to the whole neighborhood. "Do You Want This Man For A Neighbor?" That's what it says on the cover. Inside, it tells how many babies he kills in a year. It describes how young women are sometimes coerced into having abortions. The victims are encouraged to lie or to threaten suicide just so they won't have to be bothered with being pregnant. After the leaflets are passed out, we stand on the curb right in front of Dr. Meade's house and we pray. Or we sing. I don't do this because I have hate in my heart for Dr. Meade. I do it because I hate what he does. I will go there every Sunday afternoon until he stops.

Gary goes with me on Sunday afternoons. The others bring their families along too. It's like a ritual for us now – Sunday school, dinner out, then prayers at Dr. Meade's. I like having Gary along on those days. Plus you never know what to expect – we've had garden hoses turned on us and garbage thrown from cars – so I feel safer having him there. He comes by here some days, when he can. But he works hard to support us so that I can spend my time doing the Lord's work.

I do enjoy the times when he can be here. God's army needs many soldiers. We appreciate all the support we can get. Or at least we try to be appreciative. I'll admit that sometimes I get irritated with the people who show up and start telling us what to do. We've been at this for years now. We know exactly what we're doing.

And I know it is not right to say so, but I get especially bothered when the person telling us what to do is a woman without children of her own. Oh, I do understand that some women are just not able to conceive a child, but many of them have simply decided not to give birth because children would interfere with their life or their jobs.

Every time one of them comes in here, acting like she owns the place and talking about what we should and shouldn't be doing, every time that happens I just want to say, "When you know what it's like to feel a little life squirming around in your belly and when you know what it's like to spend hours in excruciating pain and when you know what it's like to be spread-eagled in some delivery room with strangers staring at your hoo-hoo, then you can tell me about how things should and should not work here."

There are days when.... *(shouts)* YOUR BABY IS GOD'S CREATION! "FOR THOU DIDST FORM MY INWARD PARTS, THOU DIDST KNIT ME TOGETHER IN MY MOTHER'S WOMB!"...there are days when my throat hurts and my feet get swollen from standing... *(shouts)* YOU ARE DOING A DISHONOR TO YOUR CREATOR! But, in general, the time passes rather quickly.

It isn't difficult to stay motivated.

I have seen pictures of whole dumpsters full of murdered babies. I will not call them fetuses. That's just a fancy word to make you forget what they are. They are babies. Plain and simple. And they deserve to have a life.

We keep some of these pictures on hand – actual photographs of preborn babies who have perished in the abortion mills. When we're doing our sidewalk counseling, we show the pictures to the women who come here. We show the pictures and we share the facts with them – tell them about all the women who have abortions and then suffer from anxiety and guilt and worse things like suicidal impulses and drug abuse. It's called post-abortion syndrome and it's a medically-proven fact. Sometimes during our sidewalk counseling, Bree gives them a model of an unborn baby that they can hold in their hands. They can see the little fingers and toes. The eyelashes. And a lot of them changes their minds right then and there.

There are thousands of babies alive today because of sidewalk counselors. I consider myself a preborn baby's last line of defense from the holocaust.

Some people don't like what we're doing here. The so-called feminists say this is about a woman's right to choose what happens to her body. But does she have the right to choose what happens to her baby's body? No. Only the Lord in heaven can make that choice.

If these feminists thought about it, they'd understand how they need to be fighting for the rights of unborn women as well. They would see how important it is to work for a world in which women could combine children and career and would not feel forced to make a disastrous choice like this one.

The feminists come by here quoting from Emma Goldman and Gloria Steinem and people like that. Why, one of their big heroes, Elizabeth Cady Stanton, said how degrading it was that women see their children as property that can just be disposed of. She said it during some women's suffrage speech she gave. But you don't see many of them quoting her, do you? No, they pick and choose the words they use to support their stand.

Occasionally someone – usually some reporter – will ask me if I think it's right to kill the doctors who perform these executions. I most certainly do not think that killing is right. Ever. Not under normal circumstances. But these are not normal circumstances. This is mass murder. And Genesis is quite clear on the subject of murder. "Whoever sheds the blood of man, by man shall his blood be shed." By *man*.

I could not do it myself, mind you. I do not have it in me to take a life. Gary says there is not a cruel bone in my body but.... *(shouts)* YOU DON'T HAVE THE RIGHT TO DO WRONG!...I just think I'm needed here to keep waging the war. The Lord needs me on the front line and not in some prison. He has made that abundantly clear to me.

Yesterday I did mention it to Gary. I told him how I believe somebody needs to step forward. He said he'd consider it but he isn't so sure he wants to make the sacrifice. Gary, I said, what's a personal sacrifice if it saves even one more little lamb for Jesus? It's not like I wouldn't have to sacrifice too. I told him that. I said I would truly hate to make do without him. Although I do like the idea of being married to a true Christian hero.

In the meantime, I will be right here. Rain, shine, sleet, or snow. Restraining order or not. I'll keep coming here – day after day, week after week – until the killing stops. And the Lord will be right here beside me. Right here.

(begins writing in notebook) J...J...Y...two...two...seven.

PLAYING THE GAME

(**STEPHANIE** *sits on a bench in front of an open locker. She wears baseball pants, a T-shirt and socks. As she speaks, she puts on her jersey and shoes.*)

Putting on your uniform is like a ritual. Like a religious ceremony. You have to do it a special way, the same way each time.

Ladie's baseball they're calling it. The all-girls team. Other teams listed us on their schedules like that. Like some exhibition or a novelty act. Or like in that movie with Madonna where the players wear little skirts or do the splits going after a fly ball. That's what people seem to expect. They're disappointed when we show up looking like every other team in the league.

Reporters talk to us and they treat us like clowns or like some kind of freaks of nature. One of them asked Marcy, our right fielder, if she likes boys or not. He actually said that. Turned his little tape recorder off and said, "Between you and me, Marcy, what's the deal? Do you like boys or not?" And Marcy looked right at him and said, "No, I do not like boys." And this reporter guy leaned back against the locker and looked all smug like he had just gotten the scoop of the century. And Marcy reached out and grabbed Jimmy Olson by the balls. Seriously. She grabbed him right by the nuts – real hard – and said, "I do not like boys. I like men. Let me know if you run into any." And she must have given him a squeeze or something because he let out this little tiny "Oh" sound and then Marcy just walked away. Jesus.

I grew up playing softball. You know, in the girls softball league where you get pastel colored jerseys and you're encouraged not to play too rough or someone could get

hurt and you get fed that "we're all winners here" crap.
Our batting helmets had flowers on them. Honest to God.
And it wasn't long before I figured out that I could hit the
ball harder, throw longer and run faster than any of the
other little girls on the team. Playing ball was clearly what
I did best. Some of the parents complained that I was too
good and that I was ruining the game for their daughters.
None of the girls on the team said this, of course. We went
along with the grown-ups with the "there are no winners
or losers stuff" but secretly we talked about pulverizing the
other team. About how we wanted to hurt them. Crush
them. We tried to put spells on their batters and one time
my teammates gave me a dollar apiece to hit the other
team's pitcher with a line drive. I made seventeen dollars.

My folks looked into having me play Little League and I
actually did get to play in two games but then a group of
parents objected and I had to quit. The boys on the team
didn't care that I was there. They wanted to play and they
wanted to win and I was helping them do that. It was the
parents who didn't want to see me out there. They said
they were afraid that I'd get hurt but I think the fact that I
hit a home run and two doubles in my first game had a lot
to do with it.

I played softball in high school. Got a scholarship to college.
And sometime during my junior year I started noticing
how all the guys on the baseball team are talking about
where they want to play and which minor league teams get
the biggest crowds and what kind of contract they'll try to
negotiate and I start thinking to myself, I start thinking,
Jesus, these guys are going to be able to keep playing and
what do I have ahead of me? An eight-to-five job and a softball league where I'll be on the same team with a bunch of
out-of-shape old P.E. majors who just want to get the game
over with so they can go drink beer? Back to playing for fun
and "we're all winners here"?

When I heard that someone wanted to start a women's
team, I was all over it. Came to the tryouts. Made the team.
And now I'm doing what I want to do. Everybody is all for

you finding a job where you get to do what you do best. Well, I've found that job. Took some adjustments, going from softball to baseball, but I used to work out with the guys on the baseball team in college so it came pretty easily to me.

We lost our first game nineteen to nothing. A lot of people thought that meant we shouldn't be playing. But that same night, the Angels lost fourteen-zip to the A's and I didn't see anyone talking about how *they* should pack it in, give it up, get "real" jobs.

(**STEPHANIE** *has finished tying her shoes. She stands and gets her glove and cap from her locker.*)

The important thing is, I guess, that it's not some women's thing for me. I am not out to make a point. To demand my rights. None of that. I just want to play. It's what I do.

After every game there's a whole crowd of kids who wait to get autographs. Boys *and* girls. All ages. And I like it because they look at me and they see me for exactly what I am. A ball player. That's all I want. I just want to play the game.

(**STEPHANIE** *puts on her cap.*)

MAMA'S HERE

(**ALICE** *sits on a plain, wooden bench. She is in her 50s or 60s and is dressed in a matronly flowered dress. She holds her purse in front of her. She wears a modest hat. Her shoes are worn but have been polished. It is obvious that she is dressed for some occasion. A clock ticks in the background.*)

I wouldn't have missed this for the world. I told Clifford, there are occasions in life when a mother just has to be there for her child. Birthdays, first day of school, first date, graduation. Days you wouldn't dream of missing for all the tea in China. Days when you have to be there for your little girl. Even when she's not so little anymore.

Candace was twenty-eight on her last birthday. Didn't mean she wasn't too old for her mama to throw her a party. A big wing-ding. We rented the Elks' lodge, hired a disk jockey, the whole shebang. People danced until three a.m. Lots of them said it was the best party they'd ever been to. Folks still talk about it. Oh, we had a fine time and Candace... Candace had the time of her life. Laughing and dancing and carrying on. It made me so happy to be her mother.

Sometimes things don't turn out exactly the way you plan them. Things happen that we wouldn't choose. But that's all part of being a parent. I remember when Candace turned eighteen. She got a tattoo. Right here on her shoulder blade. A big peace sign with flowers all wound around it. Candace – I said – this is the eighties. The hippies are all dead and gone. She told me she thought it looked "cool" and that her best friend Judy had one just like it on her fanny. I'll have to admit, it did have pretty colors to it and I was relieved that it wasn't on her behind because that always seemed so cheap to me. But still – I asked her – I said, Candace, what are your grandchildren going to think someday about havin' a grandma with a peace sign there on her back? What will they think about nana havin' a tattoo? She didn't have an answer for that one. Of course, the way it turned out....

(She drifts off for a moment, then looks at her watch.)

Ten more minutes. *(She sighs deeply and leans back on the bench. Then she sits upright. Her voice is quiet and controlled. She is almost without affect.)* Tell you what. I am so glad it's the gas chamber here. That lethal injection? What kind of thing is that? Just like goin' to sleep from what I hear. Oh sure, it stops your lungs. Stops your heart. But so what? You're out cold. You don't know the difference.

Reason why I like the gas chamber is it's supposed to be quite painful. You can't breathe, you know you're dying, you know it'll help to breathe deep and get it over with, only your lungs know that the gas hurts and they don't want any part of it so they don't let you take a deep breath. It's a very slow process. I read somewhere that the longest one took eleven minutes. That's some kind of record though. Usually it's shorter. Four minutes, five. But it seems as how that would be long enough that maybe you could remember. Remember how you got yourself there in the first place.

That's what I want him to do. Remember. When they strap him down tight to that chair, I want him to remember how it was he happened to choose her. Out of all those other girls it could have been, why her? And when they slam that door and seal it shut, I want him to remember her just as she was – an ordinary girl. Except to me, of course. I thought she was beautiful. I told her that all the time. You are my beautiful girl. She said I only thought that because I was her mother.

(She sits thinking of Candace and smiling. Gradually her smile fades.)

I want him to remember how she screamed and fought. How she dug her nails into his face and peeled the skin right off of him. I want him to think real hard about that when he hears those pellets drop into that pan of acid. When he starts to smell that rotten egg smell. Yes, I want him remembering every moment.

I do hope we can see his face. Because I want him to look me right in the eyes. I want him to see Candace's face in my face. Everybody said she was the spitting image of me. I want him to see me watching while he struggles and chokes and foams at the mouth. I want him to take the look of my face right to Hell with him.

(She opens her purse and removes a handkerchief.)

Yes, there are times in life that you just cannot miss. There are some occasions when you simply have to be there for your child.

(She gently blots her neck with the handkerchief.)

TOUCHSTONE

(**JUNE** *wears surgical scrubs.*)

The human skin is comprised of two layers. The lower layer, the dermis, houses blood vessels, sweat glands, nerve endings, and hair follicles. The outer layer, the epidermis, is covered with dead cells, which are constantly being sloughed off. These dead cells cover a layer of living epithelial cells. As the cells complete their short life cycle, the living cells push the dead ones to the surface where they are ignominiously cast off.

We are covered in twenty square feet of skin. This skin is the largest organ in the human body. Not the brain, not the lungs, not the intestines. The skin. It provides a barrier from harmful bacteria, cushions and protects the tissues and organs, heats us and keeps us cool, gives us our shape, protects us from the sun's rays.

The skin of the adolescent erupts in angry pustules and pimples. In middle age, the skin loosens and we sag in unexpected and unwanted places. The skin grows wrinkled and must be covered with lotions and creams or snipped and pulled and tucked back into smoothness. Yet for all its seeming disloyalty, the skin serves as our protector. It keeps the rain out and the warmth in. It prevents the pollutants and poisons and toxins of everyday life from invading our bodies.

Two millimeters are all that stand between our tissues and organs and the world. Between us and them. Between you and me. The skin harbors the sensation of touch. Touch is the first sense to develop in the newborn infant. It is one of the final senses to fade as we approach death. Touch by another living being is sought out, is craved, by all animals. Touch is perhaps the most talked about of all the senses.

As in touch-tone telephone. Touchstone. Touched in the head. Do not touch. Touché.

With the multitude of advances in medical technology, these *(holds up her hands)* remain the nurse's most important tool. They function both as diagnostic instrument and as powerful medicine.

A fold of skin that does not spring back after a gentle pinch may mean that a patient is dehydrated. Pale, cold, clammy skin could be caused by the peripheral vasoconstriction that accompanies shock. An area that's reddened like sunburn but remains cool to the touch indicates lack of circulation and alerts the nurse that her patient might be headed toward pressure sores.

Touchstone.

Beyond the use of touch in patient assessment, there is the use of touch to console and to reassure. To calm and to soothe. To let a patient know that they are valued as a human being.

In my training, we were taught the importance of touch. We were taught to use it to assess and to evaluate. We were taught the nurturing value of touch. I assumed that the patients expected, even welcomed, this touch. That they would sit in their rooms waiting for the healing warmth of a student nurse's hand. It did not take me long to determine that this was not always the case. That I had to become a barometer for reading the signals of my patients.

It is critical for me to recognize when a patient does not wish to be touched. I can read it in the way they shrink back or in the way their body stiffens under my hand. Sometimes the signs are there before I've even put my hand on them. A woman who keeps her purse under the blanket with her. A man with the sheets tucked up under his chin or who insists that the curtain remain drawn around his bed. In whatever way they choose, they pull away and this is my signal to do the same. To touch someone who does not wish to be touched is to force them to feel – to connect – at a time when they do not want to feel this connection. To force them to feel care and concern when they are feeling unloved. And unlovable. These are the patients – the people – who so clearly need to be touched. Yet –

Do not touch.

There are times when I can tell that a patient needs to make that connection with another being. They need it, but they don't know how to ask for it. They're embarrassed by this need, feel it makes them seem weak. Childish. With these people, I find some way to touch them and pass it off as a medical assessment. I take a pulse and hold a hand a little longer than necessary. Or I touch a forehead or squeeze a foot, ostensibly to check circulation or measure muscle tone. Maybe some of them know what I'm up to. But no one has ever questioned it or complained. Usually they relax. Their breathing becomes more regular. Sometimes they close their eyes and drift off to sleep. It's satisfying to give someone the reassurance they need while allowing them to remain in control.

After a patient has died, I make a point of touching them in some way. I hold a hand or pat a cheek. Sometimes I tousle the hair of a young child. This does nothing for them. I know that. They are long past the moment of feeling. But this final touch helps me to say good-bye and to let go. And then move on to the next patient. And the one after that.

The time moves so quickly. The patients come and go. One billion skin cells are discarded daily. Skin that felt a mother's hand, a lover's kiss, a child's tickle is literally here today and gone tomorrow.

Touch. And go.

OTHER TITLES AVAILABLE FROM SAMUEL FRENCH

DEAR MRS. MARTIN

Kate Aspengren

Comedy / 2f / Interior

Barbara Martin is surprised when her new cleaning woman, Gloria, begins writing her personal notes stories about her son who plays football for an inept team and becomes a hero when he catches his cleats in his pants and cartwheels over the goal line or about her trips to her psychic and her belief in an afterlife. Barbara gets caught up in the letter writing and a warm friendship develops between these two women from different social and economic spheres. When Barbara's husband dies unexpectedly, it is Gloria who is able to provide support and understanding. Told through Barbara's and Gloria's letters, Dear Mrs. Martin is a play about friendship, family, grief and hope.

FLYER

Kate Aspengren

Drama / 4m, 5f (to play 21 roles) / Unit Set

While the Project Mercury astronauts carried America's hopes and dreams into space, NASA was busy training another elite corps of pilots, some with more flight experience than John Glenn and company. None of this group soared into space; they were women and here is their story. *Flyer* focuses on the hopes and dreams of one young pilot in particular. Fran Douglas rises above family scorn and her fiancee's condescension to join the women's corps. Action scenes involving NASA, Congress and Fran's family are intertwined with dream sequences about an intrepid black barnstormer, Bessie Coleman, who died in the 1920s performing an aerial feat. Bessie warns Fran about the many obstacles she will have to overcome to achieve her dream, a dream left unfulfilled when NASA pulled the plug on training women for space flight.

"This story needed to be told and Ms. Aspengren tells it brilliantly." – *The Westsider*

OTHER TITLES AVAILABLE FROM SAMUEL FRENCH

HOUSE OF WONDERS

Kate Aspengren

Comedy / 3m, 5f / Interior

Holly Edwards' teen novels are so popular that her publisher has commissioned her to write an adult book for the Famous Foremothers series. Holly tries to write about her great aunt who was a madam in Alaska but soon realizes that all she knows about Myrta Jane Wonders are some old family stories. She employs a Ouija board to summon the long dead madam, who proceeds to set her niece straight about the afterlife before helping with the book. Myrta returns with her ex husband, reputedly a gangster, and two women who allegedly worked at Myrta's House of Wonders. Problems arise when these visitors do not conform to Holly's expectations. *House of Wonders* provides a hilarious look at the evolution of family stories and a unique, uplifting view of the next life.

MOTHER'S DAY

Kate Aspengren

Drama / 4f / Unit Set

Victoria accidently learned that she was adopted when she was thirteen. Now an adult, she is still angry with her adoptive mother and has discovered the identity of birth mother. After meeting her, Victoria is able to begin a reconciliation with the woman who raised her. *Mother's Day* is a touching and sensitive play about the personal journeys of three women.

OTHER TITLES AVAILABLE FROM SAMUEL FRENCH

EXCEPTIONAL MONOLOGUES 1
FOR MEN AND WOMEN

In an effort to foster awareness of new plays, and provide for the ever-constant need of audition material, Samuel French is proud to announce a new series of monologue books highlighting the latest Samuel French publications. Each year, starting with 2008, monologues from or most recent publications will be selected by our editorial staff to be included in that year's collection. Complete with play synopses, a thematic index, and broad range of styles, you are sure to find one that suits your audition needs. It's wonderful way to sample the latest Samuel French publications, too.

Exceptional Monologues 1 includes such titles and authors as: *Eurydice* by Sarah Ruhl, *The Receptionist* by Adam Bock, *In the Continuum* by Danai Gurira & Nikkole Salter, *Bach at Leipzig* by Itamar Moses, and many more.

Lightning Source UK Ltd.
Milton Keynes UK
UKOW030815060213

205883UK00007B/118/P